DEVO

PRAYER TO

SAINT MARY OF

EGYPT

Unfailing 9 Days Powerful
Prayers to Saint Mary of Egypt

CHARLOTTE SMITH

Introduction

Welcome to this novena book dedicated to
Saint Mary of Egypt, a remarkable figure in
Christian history. Born in Egypt in the 4th
century, Mary of Egypt is highly venerated
as a Desert Mother in the Eastern Orthodox
and Coptic Churches and is celebrated by
the Catholic Church as a patron saint of
penitents.

Throughout the centuries, Saint Mary of
Egypt's life story has served as a source of
inspiration and guidance for countless
faithful individuals seeking spiritual renewal
and transformation. Her unwavering
devotion, repentance, and asceticism make
her a beacon of hope for those seeking
reconciliation with God and a deeper

understanding of the power of grace and redemption.

In this novena book, we invite you to join us in a nine-day's journey of prayer, reflection, and contemplation centered on the life and legacy of Saint Mary of Egypt. Through the timeless wisdom of her experiences, we hope to draw closer to God, seek forgiveness for our shortcomings, and embrace a renewed sense of faith, love, and compassion.

As we embark on this spiritual pilgrimage, may the profound example of Saint Mary of Egypt serve as a guiding light, illuminating our path and inspiring us to deepen our relationship with God and embrace the transformative power of repentance and grace. Join us as we lift our hearts and minds in prayer, seeking Saint Mary's intercession and the blessings of spiritual renewal in our lives.

May this novena book be a source of solace, strength, and renewal as we honor and invoke the intercession of Saint Mary of Egypt, a beloved saint whose life continues to inspire and uplift the hearts of believers around the world.

Brief History

Life

Mary of Egypt, also recognized as Maria Aegyptiaca, hailed from the Egyptian Province and absconded from her parents at the tender age of twelve, relocating to Alexandria. She led a profoundly debauched existence, declining payment for her sexual services despite an insatiable urge, subsisting primarily through begging and occasional spinning of flax.

After living such a life for seventeen years, Mary journeyed to Jerusalem during the Great Feasts of the Exaltation of the Holy Cross, seeking to indulge her lust further amidst the pilgrim crowds. She paid her way with sexual favors, continuing her habits even in Jerusalem. However, when she was barred from entering the Church of the Holy Sepulchre due to her impurity, she was struck with remorse. Seeking forgiveness, she vowed to renounce her worldly ways and become an ascetic. Upon praying before an icon of the Virgin Mary, she was granted entry into the church. Prompted by a divine voice, she then sought solace in the monastery of Saint John the Baptist, where she received absolution and Holy Communion. The next day, she journeyed into the desert to live a life of penitence as a hermit, sustained only by what she could find in the wilderness.

About a year before her passing, Mary of Egypt encountered Zosimas of Palestine in the desert, where she appeared disheveled and nearly unrecognizable. Requesting his mantle for modesty, she shared her life story with him. She asked for Holy Communion the next year on Holy Thursday at the Jordan River, miraculously walking across the water to receive it. She then instructed Zosimas to meet her again in the desert the following Lent.

The following year, Zosimas journeyed to the place of their previous meeting, a twenty-day trek from his monastery. There, he discovered Mary's lifeless body with an inscription nearby indicating her passing the night he administered Holy Communion. Her body, untouched by decay, was miraculously transported to that spot. Zosimas buried her with the help of a passing lion, then shared her remarkable story with his fellow monks upon returning to the monastery. It was passed down orally until recorded by Sophronius.

Date of death

Saint Mary of Egypt, also known as Maria Aegyptica or Maria Aegyptiaca, is believed to have passed away on April 1, around 522 AD. Her feast day is celebrated on April 1st across Eastern Orthodox, Roman Catholic, and various Christian denominations.

Born in the late 5th century, Saint Mary lived a life marked by great sinfulness until a transformative encounter with the Virgin Mary led her to renounce her past and embrace a life of penance and prayer in the Egyptian desert.

For almost half a century, Saint Mary endured the rigors of desert life, facing severe challenges and temptations. Relying on wild plants and occasional offerings from travelers, she persisted in prayer and penance, seeking forgiveness for her previous transgressions.

As word of her remarkable devotion spread, pilgrims sought her counsel and prayers. Despite her solitude, Saint Mary's profound humility and repentance continued to inspire others, drawing them closer to God.

Saint Mary of Egypt is revered as an emblem of repentance and transformation, showcasing the profound impact of God's grace and compassion. Christians worldwide honor her feast day with deep reverence, recognizing her as a potent advocate and guardian saint for those seeking forgiveness and renewal.

Intercession

The intercession of Saint Mary of Egypt is a widely recognized practice in the Eastern Orthodox Church. Saint Mary of Egypt is revered for her life of repentance and asceticism in the desert, and many believers turn to her for intercession and guidance in times of need.

Saint Mary of Egypt is believed to intercede on behalf of those seeking deliverance from sinful habits, especially those related to lust and sexual temptation. Her life story, in which she overcame a life of licentiousness and devoted herself to prayer and penitence in the wilderness, serves as a source of inspiration for those struggling with similar challenges. Additionally, Saint Mary of

Egypt is often invoked for intercession in matters related to addiction, specifically for those seeking freedom from the bondage of addictive behaviors.

Here are five common intercessions often said to Saint Mary of Egypt:

1. **Protection from impure thoughts and temptations:** Many believers seek Saint Mary of Egypt's intercession when struggling with impure thoughts or facing temptations of a sexual nature. They ask for her help in resisting these temptations and maintaining purity of heart and mind.

2. **Deliverance from addiction:** Saint Mary of Egypt is often invoked by those who are battling addiction, whether it be to alcohol,

drugs, or other vices. Believers ask for her intercession in finding the strength and courage to overcome their addictions and live a life free from their destructive influence.

3. **Guidance in the pursuit of repentance and spiritual transformation:** Those seeking to turn away from a life of sin and pursue a path of repentance and spiritual growth often pray for Saint Mary of Egypt's intercession. They ask for her help in finding the strength to follow her example of radical conversion and dedication to a life of prayer and penance.

4. **Healing from the wounds of past sins:** Many individuals experience deep emotional and spiritual wounds as a result of their past

mistakes and sinful behaviors. They turn to Saint Mary of Egypt for intercession, seeking healing and restoration from the scars of their past sins.

5. **Prayers for the conversion of sinners:** Believers often ask for Saint Mary of Egypt's intercession in their prayers for the conversion of those who are caught in lives of sin and despair. They entrust the souls of these individuals to her care, hoping that through her prayers, they may experience a similar transformation as Saint Mary did in her own life.

Overall, Saint Mary of Egypt's intercession is sought by many who are in need of spiritual support and guidance, particularly in the areas of repentance, purity, and deliverance from sinful habits. Her life serves as a powerful testimony to the transformative grace of God and the possibility of radical conversion for all who turn to Him in sincere repentance.

Reflections

Reflection 1:

Saint Mary of Egypt's transformation from a life of sin and indulgence to a life of repentance and devoted faith teaches us about the power of redemption. It demonstrates that no matter what our past may be, it is never too late to seek forgiveness and pursue a life of virtue. In our personal lives, this reflection encourages us to let go of guilt and despair, and embrace the hope of transformation and renewal.

Reflection 2:

Mary's life of solitude in the desert illustrates the importance of self-reflection and introspection. In today's fast-paced and noisy world, finding moments of solitude to reflect on our thoughts, actions, and spiritual well-being is essential. Emulating Mary's dedication to solitude can help us find clarity, strengthen our faith, and foster a deeper connection with our inner selves and with God.

Reflection 3:

Saint Mary's perseverance in resisting temptations in the desert serves as a powerful reminder of the ongoing spiritual battles we face in our lives. Her story urges us to remain vigilant and steadfast in the face of worldly temptations and distractions. This reflection challenges us to cultivate discipline, self-control, and spiritual resilience as we navigate our own journey of faith and personal growth.

Reflection 4:

Mary's unwavering commitment to repentance and penitence reveals the transformative power of genuine contrition. Her life teaches us that true repentance involves not only asking for forgiveness but also actively turning away from our sinful ways. Embracing this reflection in our personal lives calls us to engage in sincere soul-searching, acknowledge our imperfections, and take concrete steps toward positive change and spiritual growth.

Reflection 5:

The depth of Mary's humility and the manner in which she willingly bore the hardships of her life in the desert exemplify the virtues of humility and endurance. Incorporating these virtues into our lives means recognizing our limitations, embracing a spirit of selflessness, and facing life's challenges with steadfastness and grace. Mary's example encourages us to approach our difficulties with humility and to seek strength and resilience through our faith.

Reflection 6:

Saint Mary's story reflects the profound impact of forgiveness on one's spiritual journey. Her encounter with the monk Zosimas and his compassionate forgiveness illustrates the transformative power of mercy. Embracing forgiveness in our personal lives means letting go of grudges and resentments, extending grace to others, and seeking reconciliation. Just as Mary's encounter with Zosimas brought her peace, forgiveness can lead us to inner healing and spiritual freedom.

Reflection 7:

Mary's unwavering trust in divine providence and her reliance on God's guidance serve as an inspirational testimony of faith. Her story challenges us to deepen our trust in God's plan for our lives, especially in times of uncertainty and adversity. By nurturing a profound sense of faith, we can cultivate a resilient spirit, find solace in times of trouble, and experience a profound sense of peace and purpose in our lives.

Reflection 8:

The story of Saint Mary of Egypt highlights the transformative power of conversion and spiritual awakening. Her journey from a life of sin to one of holiness reminds us that true change is possible through faith and the grace of God. Embracing this reflection involves being open to spiritual growth, seeking a deeper relationship with God, and remaining receptive to the transformative work of the Holy Spirit in our lives.

Reflection 9:
Mary's life of prayer and devotion emphasizes the importance of cultivating a vibrant and consistent prayer life. Her dedication to prayer in the desert underscores the value of communing with God, seeking His presence, and aligning our hearts with His will. Integrating this reflection into our personal lives involves prioritizing regular prayer, fostering a deeper

spiritual connection, and finding strength and guidance through intimate communion with God.

In summary, the life of Saint Mary of Egypt offers us rich reflections that resonate in our personal lives by inspiring us to embrace the hope of redemption, prioritize self-reflection and solitude, persevere in the face of temptation, practice genuine repentance, embody humility and endurance, extend and receive forgiveness, deepen our faith, pursue spiritual transformation, and cultivate a vibrant prayer life. Incorporating these reflections into our lives can lead to profound spiritual growth, resilience, and a deeper sense of connection with God.

9 DAYS NOVENA PRAYER TO SAINT MARY OF EGYPT

(Begin with the sign of the Cross, Precede with an opening Prayer, Say the Prayer and silently ask your personal intentions. Conclude each day by reciting one Our Father... one Hail Mary... one Glory Be...)

Day One

O Saint Mary of Egypt, you spent many years in a life of sin, but when the Lord called you to repentance, you responded with a fervent heart. Like the woman who wept at the feet of Jesus, you shed tears of sorrow for your sins. Intercede for us, that we may recognize our own need for God's mercy and have the courage to turn away from sin. Help us to seek the Lord with all our hearts, just as you did in the desert. Amen.

(Mention your request here…)

Saint Mary of Egypt, pray for us.
Amen.

Say 1: Our Father ... Say 1: Hail Mary ...
Say 1: Glory be ...

NOTES

_____

_____

_____

_____

_____

_____

_____

_____

_____

_____

_____

_____

Day Two

Dear Saint Mary of Egypt, you embraced a life of solitude in the desert, seeking God with a pure and earnest heart. Through your intercession, may we find the strength to detach ourselves from worldly distractions, to create space for seeking deeper communion with God. Help us to prioritize our relationship with the Lord and to seek Him in prayer and contemplation. Pray for us, that we may cultivate a spirit of humility and penance in our lives. Amen.

(Mention your request here…)

Saint Mary of Egypt, pray for us.
Amen.

Say 1: Our Father ... Say 1: Hail Mary ...
Say 1: Glory be ...

NOTES

_____

_____

_____

_____

_____

_____

_____

_____

_____

_____

_____

_____

_____

Day Three

Saint Mary of Egypt, you experienced the transforming power of God's grace in the depths of the desert. Through your intercession, may we too be open to the workings of God in our lives, allowing His grace to heal and transform us. Help us to trust in God's providence and to surrender ourselves fully to His will. Pray for us, that we may experience the freedom and joy that comes from living in accordance with God's divine plan for our lives. Amen.

(Mention your request here...)

Saint Mary of Egypt, pray for us.
Amen.

Say 1: Our Father ... Say 1: Hail Mary ...
Say 1: Glory be ...

NOTES

_____

_____

_____

_____

_____

_____

_____

_____

_____

_____

_____

Day Four

O Saint Mary of Egypt, you endured great physical and spiritual hardships in the desert, yet you remained steadfast in your pursuit of holiness. Through your intercession, may we find the courage and perseverance to endure our own trials and tribulations. Help us to trust in God's mercy and to hold fast to our faith, even in the face of adversity. Pray for us, that we may be strengthened in our resolve to follow Christ, no matter the challenges we may encounter. Amen.

(Mention your request here…)

Saint Mary of Egypt, pray for us.
Amen.

Say 1: Our Father ... Say 1: Hail Mary ...
Say 1: Glory be ...

NOTES

Day Five

Dear Saint Mary of Egypt, you encountered the monk Zosimas in the desert, and through your witness, he was inspired to renew his commitment to the Lord. Through your intercession, may we too be a source of inspiration to others, leading them closer to Christ through our words and actions. Help us to be beacons of hope and encouragement to those who are struggling in their faith. Pray for us, that we may be instruments of God's love and mercy in the lives of others. Amen.

(Mention your request here…)

Saint Mary of Egypt, pray for us.
Amen.

Say 1: Our Father ... Say 1: Hail Mary ...
Say 1: Glory be ...

NOTES

_____

_____

_____

_____

_____

_____

_____

_____

_____

_____

_____

_____

Day Six

O Saint Mary of Egypt, you humbly shared your life story with the monk Zosimas, revealing the depths of God's mercy and forgiveness. Through your intercession, may we also be willing to open our hearts to others, sharing our own experiences of God's grace and redemption. Help us to be authentic witnesses to the power of God's love in our lives. Pray for us, that we may be instruments of spiritual renewal and healing for those around us. Amen.

(Mention your request here…)

Saint Mary of Egypt, pray for us.
Amen.

Say 1: Our Father … Say 1: Hail Mary …
Say 1: Glory be …

NOTES

_____

_____

_____

_____

_____

_____

_____

_____

_____

_____

_____

_____

Day Seven

Dear Saint Mary of Egypt, you received the Eucharist from the hands of the monk Zosimas, experiencing a deep sense of spiritual nourishment and renewal. Through your intercession, may we too approach the sacraments with reverence and awe, recognizing the profound graces that flow from them. Help us to deepen our devotion to the Eucharist and the sacrament of reconciliation, drawing strength and healing from these encounters with the Lord. Pray for us, that we may be sustained and transformed by the life-giving grace of the sacraments. Amen.

(Mention your request here…)

Saint Mary of Egypt, pray for us.

Amen.

Say 1: Our Father ... Say 1: Hail Mary ...
Say 1: Glory be ...

NOTES

_____

_____

_____

_____

_____

_____

_____

_____

_____

_____

_____

Day Eight

O Saint Mary of Egypt, you were granted a vision of the glory of heaven, and your soul was filled with an indescribable joy. Through your intercession, may we also fix our hearts and minds on the eternal rewards that await us in heaven. Help us to live each day with a sense of purpose and hope, knowing that our ultimate goal is union with God in paradise. Pray for us, that we may be inspired to live in a manner worthy of the heavenly kingdom that awaits us. Amen.

(Mention your request here…)

Saint Mary of Egypt, pray for us.
Amen.

Say 1: Our Father … Say 1: Hail Mary …
Say 1: Glory be …

NOTES

Day Nine

Dear Saint Mary of Egypt, you spent many years in repentance and prayer, seeking the mercy and forgiveness of God. Through your intercession, may we too embrace a life of ongoing conversion and spiritual growth. Help us to continually turn to the Lord in humility, seeking His guidance and grace in all aspects of our lives. Pray for us, that we may remain faithful to the path of holiness, and that we may one day rejoice with you in the eternal bliss of heaven. Amen.

(Mention your request here…)

Saint Mary of Egypt, pray for us.
Amen.

Say 1: Our Father ... Say 1: Hail Mary ...
Say 1: Glory be ...

NOTES

Made in United States
Orlando, FL
05 November 2024